A JOURNEY INTO WOMANHOOD:

The Key Guide For Millennial Woman to Achieve Success, Self-Love and Happiness

By: Krystal Davy

This book is dedicated to myself

"Continue to believe in yourself, love yourself, enjoy your life and make the world a better place" – *Mom*

Acknowledgements

God, My Mom & Dad

My Two Sisters *(Tiffany and Samantha),* **Aunts, Uncles, Cousins , Friends & Family, Hazel Shaw,** *(Thank you for being there for me in my time of need.)* **My Professors at York College** *(Ebonie Jackson, Jonathan Quash, Dr. Baron and Dr. Phelps,* & **Book Coach Jasmine Womack**

Table of Contents

Introduction

From the outside looking in, everyone looks at me as if I have made it. I'm the one that made it out, the one who has the career, apartment, job, looks and intelligence. You know that saying *don't judge a book by its cover*? I'm a reflection of that, a two sided masterpiece. Yes, on the outside you see the good, but what you don't see is how I almost lost myself through different struggles such as overcoming domestic violence, depression and anxiety at a point in my life and also a lack of self-love. If I didn't know myself and who I was, I would have never made it. In this book you'll read about my experiences and how I overcame these obstacles by the grace of God. You will also learn the key principles that I have learned in my life that will help to sustain you as a millennial and help you achieve success, self love and happiness, as you transition into womanhood. Sit back and enjoy my journey into womanhood.

Chapter 1.

~

Know God

One of the things that is most important for you to achieve success, self-love and happiness in life is your relationship with God. Your relationship with God is important. It is God who gives us the strength that guides us and takes cares of us when no one else does. I developed a sense of spirituality, faith and desire to read the Bible when I was in college. My father is a very spiritual person and he grew up reading his Bible regularly when he was younger. He would call me when I was away at Howard University and encourage me to read the Bible. He would also read certain scriptures with me. I remember reading Psalms 25 and it being the first chapter that resonated with me.

"Unto thee, O Jehovah, do I lift up my soul. O my God, in thee have I trusted, Let me not be put to shame; Let not mine enemies triumph over me. Yea, none that wait for thee shall be put to shame: They shall be put to shame that deal treacherously without cause. Show me thy ways, O Jehovah; Teach me thy paths. Guide me in thy truth, and teach me; For thou art the God of my salvation; For thee do I wait all the day. Remember, O Jehovah, thy tender mercies and thy lovingkindness; For they have been ever of old. Remember not the sins of my youth, nor my transgressions: According to thy lovingkindness remember thou me, For thy goodness' sake, O Jehovah. Good and upright is Jehovah: Therefore will he instruct sinners in the way. The meek will he guide in justice; And the meek will he teach his way. All the paths of Jehovah are lovingkindness and truth Unto such as keep his covenant and his testimonies. For thy name's sake, O Jehovah, Pardon mine iniquity, for it is great. What man is he that feareth Jehovah? Him shall he instruct in the way that he shall choose. His soul shall dwell at ease; And his seed shall inherit the land. The friendship of Jehovah is with them that fear him; And he will show them his covenant. Mine eyes are ever toward Jehovah; For he will pluck my feet out of the net. Turn thee unto me, and have mercy upon me; For I am desolate and afflicted. The troubles of my heart are enlarged: Oh bring thou me out of my distresses. Consider mine affliction and my travail; And forgive all my sins.

Oh keep my soul, and deliver me: Let me not be put to shame, for I take refuge in thee. Let integrity and uprightness preserve me, For I wait for thee. Redeem Israel, O God, Out all of his troubles."

Especially the verses that mentioned the troubles of my heart being enlarged resonated with me the most.

I remember having difficult times and also having people who didn't like me, who were envious or "enemies" without cause and to see that it was mentioned in the Bible and that the Lord would protect me from these people and situations just amazed me and I got a desire to read more and get to know the Lord.

I also saw how God began to work in my life. I wasn't in the best place of my life at the time and wasn't making all of the right decisions and as I drew closer to God, I became more focused, eliminated unnecessary drama and started to lean on Him more. I then invested in my own Bible and began to turn to it whenever I needed guidance or strength. The foundation of the Lord is unmovable and one of the greatest relationships that you can have in life.

At times being a Christian can seem challenging, but to know that God loves you unconditionally, is a comforting form of protection and it gives all the wisdom and strength needed in life. Rest in the Lord and pray always, rejoice and rest in Him. Take time out in the day to read and pray, always keep your relationship with God and make an effort to study His word and walk in His ways.

"Wisdom is the principal thing; therefore get wisdom: and with all thy getting get understanding."Proverbs 4:7 King James Version (KJV)

Chapter 2.

~

Know Thyself & Stay Grounded

I decided to write a book to tell my story. In life, like many of us, I have been blessed with many opportunities and gifts from God, but have faced a number of obstacles. I thought I would never make it through. I'm ready to share my story now because it's my time! Time to help others heal. Time to help others find the courage to get through their experiences. Time to use all I know to help other woman succeed. From the outside looking in, everyone looks at me as if I have "made it". If I didn't know myself and who I was I would have never made it.

This ladies and gentlemen is the beginning of my story. At the young age of twenty-one, I was put out of my home. I was working for a modeling agency making $100 a week and was put out of my house due to a dysfunctional relationship with my mother. Thank God we have rebuilt that relationship and it is now stronger than ever. I was always forced to do a lot for myself and put in a position where I had no choice but to learn how to work hard, make connections and do whatever I needed to do by any means necessary to succeed.

Through my experiences in life, I started to learn more about myself a young girl from the Bronx, who attended Catholic school from first through eighth grade and then and attended high school in Harlem. High school was a new experience for me as I'm sure it was for all of us. It was there where I really became social. I started dating and making friends both in school and throughout the neighborhood. I made many friends but started engaging in activities that weren't good for me.

Even though I was getting distracted socially, I always had a strong academic foundation and knew that no matter what, I had to do my work in school. After attending high school, I got accepted into my dream college, Howard University. At the time, I had the skills I needed to get good grades, but I wasn't as informed on networking, getting involved and making connections as yet. I was also 17 years old when I started my freshman year and brought the habits that I had learned with me from my neighborhood high school to college. After completing two years of college in Washington, DC, for financial reasons I came back to New York. Luckily I left with about a 3.0 grade point average and was able to transfer my credits to the next school I attended, York College, The City University of New York.

I was particularly drawn to women of color because this was missing from my life at the time. I had a void that needed to be filled. When I went to York, I was fortunate to have many professors that became mentors to me and were also honestly passionate about helping their students. I didn't share what I was going through at the time because I was working on making sure I had a career once I graduated and wanted to be known and seen as a professional at all times. I became heavily involved in activities on campus and found mentorship and guidance through the social clubs on York's campus. After attending a few events at the Women's Center, I became the president of the Women's Club and developed an impactful relationship with Ebonie Jackson, who was a role model and mentor to me. Ebonie served as the Director of the Women's Center on our college campus. She started to take me to conferences, taught me how to network and how to speak at events. She also taught me how to carry, brand and present myself as a professional.

She once told me, the ambition I have today is because of the exposure I got at Howard even though I didn't finish. I guess she was right. I mean Howard was just a different experience. Being surrounded by beautiful black people from all over the world who were there to get and education, joining all different organizations on campus and building great relationships with each other was a very impactful experience for me.

Being at York was the perfect opportunity for me. It was a small campus with HBCU ambience. After becoming the president of the Women's Club, I was introduced to Mr. Quash, the Director of the Men's Center at York, during music class. Class was engaging because we sang a lot of gospel songs which was fun for me because I liked to sing and also loved the Lord. Mr Quash gave me the opportunity to be a tutor and work to help other child in the Men's Center on our campus. This opportunity introduced me to the work of a teacher. I taught my first class through an SAT program that he ran in the Men's Center.

At York College, Jean Phelps who serves as the Director of Student Activities and Dr. Linda Michelle Baron, a professor in the Teacher Education Department both had an enormous influence on my life as well. Both women, members of Alpha Kappa Alpha Sorority, Incorporated, and faculty members at York were role models to me. I looked up to them and admired them for their character, class, ambition and passion to help others. After running for student government, I was elected to be the Parliamentarian and built a close relationship with Dr. Phelps after experiencing real politics and political division on our campus. There were people who had motives to control our school budget and were engaging in things they shouldn't have but I never engaged. She was able to see my authenticity in the work that I was doing and that I genuinely wanted to help our student body. I will never forget the moment when she told me "You will go far in life because you have integrity." Ten words that stuck with me to this day and that will always stay with me. I learned I had integrity, the meaning of it and to always uphold it. As a an education major, I also became involved in the Teacher Education Department, under the council of Dr. Baron, one of the most authentic, encouraging and inspiring professionals that I have encountered. Dr. Baron is vibrant, real and always actually about helping her students. She always engaged us through her poetry and is truly about open doors and supporting today's future leaders.

I became the President for our Teacher Education Honor Society, Kappa Delta Pi and began to work closely with Dr. Baron. These professors and experiences helped to change my life. It gave me a new outlook on life and introduced me to a new path.

I joined all the clubs that I didn't join at Howard, took advantage of all the leadership positions and any opportunities that would help me to market myself as I prepared to leave undergraduate school.

To this day, I am appreciative of the lessons I learned. I learned the importance of building personal relationships. If you want to be successful, you have to have a network. Think about who you can call when you need help with a particular task, who has a particular skill set or knowledge in a certain area that you may want to leverage, or who you can ask for advice or build ideas off of when needed. This is your network. Leverage your network and people you build personal and professional relationships with when needed.

I want you to reflect and think of the experiences that shaped you in your childhood, adolescence, and young adult and adult years. Stay grounded in these experiences and know yourself.

As women, it is important to know yourself, know your experiences, and know who you have in your corner. It's important for you to stay grounded in who you are and not let anyone or any societal influences shape who you are or who you think you should be. Everyone else is already taken so never be afraid to just be yourself.

Forget about trends, what's in and who the world is telling you to be. Be authentic. Authenticity for me was just a big thing. I would always take time to reflect on where I have been and what made me into the person I am today. Knowing who I am helps me to stay grounded.

. . .Life Will Come With A Lot of Changes As Long As You Don't Lose Yourself, You'll Win, Know Yourself. . .

Chapter 3.

$\sim$

Honor Your Parents

I'm a first generation American born to both Caribbean parents from Jamaica. It wasn't until my late 20s when I realized that my parents were my right and my left. I've always had a close relationship with my dad and even though the relationship I had with my mother wasn't the best, after a few years we began to repair it. After graduating from York College, I was fortunate to secure a full time teaching position and was able to move into my own apartment. This is when adulthood really began for me.

After transitioning into adulthood, I realized that my mom, dad and immediate family were the ones who were there for me. Think about when you have hit rock bottom. It's your mother and father who will be there for you no matter what. So many young adults and millennials pride themselves in being "independent", having friends and separating themselves from their parents but fail to realize that it's their parents who will be there for them through thick and thin because they want the best for them.

God tells us to "Honour thy father and mother; which is the first commandment with a promise;

That it may be well with thee, and thou mayest live long on the earth" Ephesians 6:1-4 King James Version (KJV)

You were born into your family for a reason. Your parents are your parents for a reason.

It is important that you listen to your parents. Think for yourself but know they want the best for you. Listen to their instinct and their insight. Hold on to the traditional values and be proud. Even if you have to be the glue that holds them together when things get tough and rough and you are on the bottom with nowhere else to go it is your family that will be the ones that are there for your first. Make an effort to build a relationship with your parents, speak to them daily and live your life in a way that would make them proud. Do things that you know are in line with what they would want for you.

I appreciate my parents from the bottom of my heart and even though things weren't perfect I know that if my back is against the wall, I can depend on them and I am happy for the morals and values that they have instilled in me as they aided in who I am today. No matter what kind of situation you're in, that person that you look at as your parent or guardian, honor them.

"Honour thy father and mother; which is the first commandment with promise; That it may be well with thee, and thou mayest live long on the earth" Ephesians 6:1-4 King James Version (KJV)

Chapter 4.

~

Embrace Family

I was fortunate enough to be born into a family of two sisters, six male cousins and many aunts and uncles and family members that I don't even now. Having male cousins, who were basically like brothers was one of the best things growing up. I always had family members around me that would protect me, that would be there to knock some common sense in my head if I needed it, that would just be there to show me unconditional love, and remind me who I was at times when I forgot.

Things aren't always the best in our family. Sometimes different family members get into arguments over small issues but it's important to remember to be the glue. Be the person that remains positive and try to resolve conflicts if possible. It's important to remember to value the people in your life and know that your family is who they are for a reason.

As mentioned before, it's important for you to honor your parents. It's also important for you embrace your family as well. A part of loving yourself is being true to yourself and keep close relationships with those around you. I've seen so many people branch out and try to fit in other circles that they do not take time to embrace their own family. I have close relationships with my cousins and family members and this has attributed to me knowing myself, being grounded in myself and being happy. People will try to tell you who you are but you can't believe them. Who else knows you better than your family? My cousins always uplifted me, protected me and helped to keep me grounded through storms and trials that I have faced. It is important that you have a support system. Not just family, but your tribe, the ones who are going to have your back, the ones that know who you genuinely are as a person when you forget who you are. The ones that are going to accompany you when everyone is busy.

Make a conscious effort to spend time with your loved ones. Think about who will not judge you or who is not looking at you in the way of the public eye? Your family will not. Build great relationships with your family. Take time out of your busy schedule to spend time with your them. Have game nights and make sure to celebrate holidays, birthdays and different occasions.

Even if it's not your immediate family, take time to get to know them. Leverage these relationships. They will bring you joy and they'll help you to stay grounded because you're not trying to fill in holes somewhere else. Receiving love from family members will help you love yourself. Now I don't want you to be naïve you will have family members that you may feel like you can't trust of course because people are human, but make sure to leverage, love and build with the ones you can.

. . . The love of family is life's greatest blessing. . .

Chapter 5.

⌇

Own Your Morals & Values

Values are the principles that people care about the most. They are what cause us to behave the way we do, think the way we think and make the decisions that we make. What are your morals? What do you value the most in life? Your morals and values are important because they help you make conscious decisions about what you want out of life based on what you believe and what you think. Many people inherit their morals and values from their family. Some are learned throughout life and surprisingly there are people who have none. Some morals and values include being kind, considerate, generous, respectful, having boundaries and standards.

Having values is extremely important. After reflecting, I am able to know the my values, I'm able to know and honor the values my parents ingrained in me. My mom is a strong woman who plays no games. Period. I get my strength from her along with my attitude for not tolerating nonsense. Being fearless when it comes to saying how I feel is also something I get from my mother. I learned to do these things with respect and humility because is important to treat people the way I want to be treated. I have also learned a lot of values from my dad. My dad taught me the importance of spirituality, how to be humble and the importance of wisdom. It is a blessing to have these morals and values instilled in me. Some people try so hard to keep up with what is going on in society that they forget who they are at the core. Own you. Own your morals. Own your values. You are important and you're what matters. Stop focusing on other people and what they're doing. When time passes, the things you're worried about or trying to keep up with, will be irrelevant. Be who you are at the core. Not the egotistical you, but the humble version of yourself. The person you are when your pure in spirit. This is the person who is grounded, who knows who they are no matter what. This is also who walks into rooms wondering if she likes the people instead of people liking her. Stay grounded, be a leader and not a follower, own who you are and let people follow you.

What are the morals and values that your family has instilled in you? My mother also instilled in me the importance of education, the importance of having confidence and the importance of self-respect. What are the values that have been instilled in you? Make sure that you uphold them no matter what. Don't let people and society shift your ideas and lower your standards and change you from what you need to be. If you're someone that lacks particular morals and values from your particular upbringing, think about someone who has been an inspiration to you. What are some things that you value about them? Learn and embrace these attributes for yourself.

I meet so many people that don't know who they are and are trying to fit into what society and what people around them say they should be like. Always embrace your own morals and values so you are grounded and you know who you are .

Especially for millennials, in today's society, there's always pressure for us to look a certain way, sound a certain way, accomplish goals by a particular time. We are all trying to balance having a career, social lives and possibly the pressure of being married or having kids by a certain age in order to appear "successful." Don't let society put pressure on you. Stay in your own lane and know who you are. Own your authentic self, your morals and values.

. . .Be Yourself, The World Will Adjust. . .

Chapter 6.

~

Guard Yourself

Have you ever heard of a really empathic person or a person that just wants to please everyone? Well that my dear friends used to be me. If I take a liking to someone, I would want them to be my best friend automatically. If I meet a guy I thought I liked, I would go to lengths to give them my all because I'm naturally really nice. If that's not enough, I was the person that would want to change the world, make everyone happy and help people be better! In this day and age that might be the worst approach known to mankind.

Over the years I've learned being too nice and thinking with emotion can stop me from making logical decisions and thinking practically. I also learned that people are not necessarily in the same place as me, sometimes just aren't on my level in all forms, and won't always have the same intentions. It's not always up to you to save the world so don't feel like you have to. As women, we naturally want to love and nurture, but in order to be our best selves, we need to guard our hearts, use mind over matter and always think practically! Men do it, so why shouldn't we?

I've been through a lot in my life. These experiences have taught me to protect myself, not out of fear but just to be wise. You can't have anyone and everyone near you. Learn who they are over a period of time. See their intentions and how they are with other people and in other situations.

You're a treasure, treat yourself as such. It's important to guard yourself and treasure yourself. It is still important to know how to be alone so you're not codependent on anyone or anything. I'm all about positivity and helping people but unfortunately, people are in different places of their life. They may be unhappy and just have different intentions. You need to guard yourself from negativity and negative people such as naysayers, backbiters, gossipers, hypocrites, energy drainers, leeches and liars.

People will try to use you for different reasons. People will try to bring you down because they're miserable and unhappy people will try to use you to benefit themself. Always keep your guard up and don't be easy to trust. A pet peeve of mine is fake people. A fake person would never be taken into my spirit. Be who you truly are in my presence and when you're not. Whatever you say behind a person's back , you should be able to say in front of them. I like to believe that the world is perfect. I like to believe that the world is a happy place. But we know that people even disliked Jesus without a cause.

In Romans 1:29-32 The Bible talks about the unjust and their ways "Being filled with all unrighteousness, fornication, wickedness, covetousness, maliciousness; full of envy, murder, debate, deceit, malignity; whisperers, Backbiters, haters of God, despiteful, proud, boasters, inventors of evil things, disobedient to parents, Without understanding, covenant breakers, without natural affection, implacable, unmerciful: Who knowing the judgment of God, that they which commit such things are worthy of death, not only do the same, but have pleasure in them that do them."

I write this to you to just be wise and be careful with people in general. Take your time getting to know people in relationships. Many men aren't usually who they are in the beginning and you start to get to know the real them over a period of time. The same thing goes for friendships, over a period of time, analyze if this person shows up for you. If they're loyal and honest it will show over time. Are they supportive? Does their energy uplift you or pull you down? These are things to think about when considering the people that you let into your life.

It is also possible to guard yourself and still be personable. You can engage with people in different ways and about different things, you can also learn how to empathize with them but still keep yourself and emotions first.

You can share some things that you may have in common or engage in general topics, but learn to keep some personal things to yourself. Sometimes privacy can be sacred, its okay if people don't know every detail about you.

Be a woman with standards so that people know in order to be in your life, they need to meet your standards. Some examples of standards to have for yourself are:

☐ Make sure whoever is in your life knows that they have to treat you with respect.

- ☐ Make sure whoever is in your life is there for you emotionally or in any other capacity.
- ☐ Set clear boundaries.
- ☐ Surround yourself with people who empower you.
- ☐ Keep people who are a positive influence in your life.

Guarding yourself as a woman is so important. Don't be so easy to trust people and let people into your life. You're precious and phenomenal and so is your life and your space. Always be mindful and cautious about moves and decisions you make. Once you know about a person and you are able to discern their spirit, you know how to move around them. You know if you can be yourself fully or maybe you need to be a little bit more guarded. Always keep your guard up and protect yourself if necessary. Not out of fear, but in using wisdom. When you do let your guard down, trust that God is in control and you've made the right decision.

. . .Guard your heart with all diligence because out of it are the issues of life. . .

Chapter 7.

~

Be Wise & Think Practically

Sometimes because of having a good heart, women can often be naive in certain situations especially when it comes to intimate relationships or situations. You need to know that not everyone thinks the way you do. People are in different places if their lives and not everyone will have a genuine and kind heart like you do. People have all had different experiences in life, but I learned that some people will internalize their experiences and begin to hurt other people they come in contact with because of things that they have experienced in their past.

Be wise and cautious when making decisions. Not everyone is for you. Trust your instincts. Don't go off of feelings and practice thinking logically and practically. I learned that it is not your responsibility to help everyone and save the world, not everyone wants to be helped. Some people are okay with not being at peace. You need to learn that not everyone will be there for you and that is okay. Remember, in these times and situations that it is not you, it's them. Stay away from these type of people. They can become draining, energy suckers, full of negativity, and will try to pull you down due to their own unhappiness.

A lot of times it is common for women to react off of emotion, but this is a habit that we need to break at times. Get in the mindset and habit of honestly not caring and save your emotions for people who are deserving and worthy of them. Be wise in all the decisions you make, whether it is professionally, personally or even intimately.

If you want to make decisions regarding business or on a professional level, you need to be strategic and think through everything that you do. You need to make sure that you are being wise and thinking practically.

If you have a dream or a vision you need to be focused; tunnel vision. Do not worry about anyone else or what they're doing, but focus on YOU! Do not think with emotions, but thinking logically and practically about every move you make! When you're focused on a dream or vision, you need a clear mind. Think Practically, your mental state is EVERYTHING.

. . .Less emotions, more practical thinking. . .

Chapter 8.

~

Mind Over Matter

ind over matter is one of my favorite phrases. It
means using will power to overcome physical prob-
lems. When you're in the worst situations, know
that even though it may feel permanent, struggle is temporary
and people cannot trap your mind. Mind over matter means
having the mental strength to believe and overcome the present.
It's about building a strong mindset, a powerful and driven focused mindset. You are what you think. Practice telling yourself
positive mantras and phrases. Be fully invested in yourself and
practice being mindful.

This also takes building a mindset in which you think forward. You're not fully focused on the present, and the troubles
that are current, but more focused mentally on where you want
to be, where you see yourself, and what you will overcome. It
takes practical thinking with less emotion and more strength. The
ability to build a strong state of mind will help you to get far in

life. You need to learn how to be strong minded, to not care about things that are irrelevant at times and how to keep your focus. You are in control of your mindset, foster it and build it.

. . .Your mind has energy make sure it has thoughts that are positive and powerful. . .

Chapter 9.

~

Don't Be Afraid to Be a Boss

Never be afraid to be a boss and never let anyone try to play you. No one. As a boss, in your personal life, don't let anyone have any expectations from you. Love yourself, you built yourself and designed yourself, there's no one like you. Always keep yourself first no matter what and put yourself in a position to need no one. Boss up.

As I mentioned before, I have been blessed to acquire my own house, car, career, and professional success. How did I get these things? Being fully transparent, I don't put anyone before me. Things that I have been through in my life have put me in the position to have to care about myself. If I don't do what needs to be done for myself, it doesn't get done. I'm all I have, so it's my responsibility to make sure I'm taking care of myself no matter what. I also don't let people have any expectations of me. Especially people who are doing little or nothing for me. Some people may perceive this as selfish but at the end of the day, you are all you have, so you need to boss up and keep yourself first.

As women, we are expected to take care of everyone, to fulfill the superwoman theory, be nurturers and healers. But who takes care of us? You have to make taking care of yourself a priority and not feel guilty about it.

You have to be confident and powerful and not feel guilty about it. I once gave a speech in undergrad about the importance of women "Leaning In." I discussed the importance of women not being afraid to step up, take on leadership roles, grab opportunities and voice their opinions without hesitation. Whenever men are confident or speak their opinions, they are known as being powerful or leaders, but when women assert themselves or are powerful, they are known as being bossy or the other B-word they like to use to describe powerful women. Don't worry about what people think and society's double standards. Don't be afraid to be a boss!

Don't be worried about people's feelings, don't be worried about people how people see you.

Learn to be more confident and don't believe every negative thought that crosses your mind. Confidence is key. You have to believe in yourself, be comfortable with making people uncomfortable and do not be afraid to be a boss!

"You're not intimidating, they are intimidated"

Chapter 10.

~

Set Boundaries & Stick to Them

Sometimes you need to be overprotective of yourself. Sometimes you need to take time to open up to people. You need to cherish yourself and know that you are as special as a gem or a diamond so anyone that you allow into your space or your life needs to bring value.

You don't have to allow yourself to be accessible to people at all times. Keep yourself guarded and let it down when you know you can. Boundaries will help to give you clarity and will continue to help you learn how to respect and love yourself.

Set boundaries with people who are not good for you. Sometimes we want to be kind to everyone and want to have peace with the world. But, it is a sad reality that not everyone prefers peace. Everyone doesn't have the same intentions, everyone is not going to be as amiable as you. Set boundaries so you can analyze the people in your life and get rid of the people that no longer need to be there.

Setting clear boundaries and spending time alone will also give you the ability to be successful. You need to learn how to be alone. Having people around you all the time can be draining, especially if you're an introverted person like I am. You need to know how to keep a balance between having social time and setting boundaries so you are able to take care of you.

Stick to the boundaries you set and know that it is okay to have them. You don't have to let everyone in and you don't have to let everyone know everything about you. Keep clear boundaries and know that a people pleasing mentality isn't healthy. It's okay for you to say NO.

. . .Setting Boundaries Is a Way of Caring For Myself. . .

Chapter 11.

~

Self-Love, Self-Respect, Self-Care

One of my biggest flats was entertaining people that aren't any good for me. I really believe that I am the living and breathing Mary Jane from the show Being Mary Jane played by Gabrielle Union-Wade. Always looking for love in all the wrong places. A living, breathing younger Mary Jane. Not just because of complexion and resemblance as many people tell me, but also experiences. Like Mary Jane, I had to learn who I am and learn how to love myself. With all the things that I have been through, if I didn't learn the importance of healing, being honest with myself and just learning to love me, I wouldn't be the woman I am today. Life will come at you but have to know the game of life. You have to build your resistance. You're the only one that matters, at times all you will have is you. Spending time alone can be rewarding, give you peace of mind and bring great comfort. You're a dynamic woman, a work in progress, always be kind to yourself. Do things you love, live in the moment, enjoy life and you!

I have been blessed in many areas of my life. I have been blessed with success. I have been blessed with beauty and intelligence. I have even been blessed with acquiring physical luxuries in my life, but my biggest flaw in life is entertaining men that I have no reason to talk to. Men who are not on my level, men who pursued me that I should have never give the time of day to. Men who wasted my time or once they achieve a certain goal, they decided to leave me alone, do a 180, turn their back and no longer talk to me, or no longer be the nice person that they were in the beginning.

I've seen men who are so selfish they even put themselves before their children. They pride themselves in having no emotions and being players even after the age of 30.

Then there are the men who have acquired everything in life. They are the successful men who have the house, the car, the career. The man that you think any woman would want to be with. Later on you find out that because of his ego and insecurity, he's he's unable to support your goals and dreams. He wants someone who is going to support him and his ego, but doesn't know how to reciprocate.

He can't deal with the fact that a woman is just a strong or just as successful as he is so as a result, he doesn't know how to treat her. How is a man going to know how to treat you if he doesn't even know how to love himself?

As women, we need to analyze the character of the men that

we date. That is what matters, not a male's looks, not what he has, but how he treats people. A man's character on the inside is what determines who he really is. Some men have deep trust issues, unresolved issues, and the way they treat people is probably a result of an internal battle that they are facing and it has nothing to do with you. Repeat this and know this: "*It has nothing to do with me*" It took me a long time to realize this. Let's face it some people are just crazy.

You should be with someone who knows how to communicate, respectful, supportive of your goals, faithful, and who makes you feel safe. Wait for the right person. The right person will come if it is God's will. The right person will give you peace, the right person will elevate you, and not pull you down. He should also be someone who is genuine and kind to others. Even if you're single, enjoy this time alone. Use this time to learn about yourself, do things you enjoy and build closer relationships with friends and family.

Take time to practice self care. Some examples of things that you can do include:

- ☐ breathing exercises
- ☐ hair wash days
- ☐ manicures and pedicures
- ☐ hanging out with people who make you feel good
- ☐ watching your favorite TV show
- ☐ cleaning the house
- ☐ aromatherapy

- ☐ a bubble bath
- ☐ listening to music
- ☐ taking yourself out on a date
- ☐ shopping

Practice keeping yourself first because at the end of the day you are all you have. Practice being calm, practice being at ease, practice being happy in life, practice loving yourself.

I really find pleasure in spending time alone. Practicing self love helps me to find my inner peace. Make it a habit, even if it's once a week, to find that alone time and continue to love yourself.

> *"Self care and self-love are not selfish, it's how you take your power back"*

Chapter 12.

~

Healing

As I said, one my biggest flaws in the past was entertaining guys that weren't any good for me. I didn't really have anything in common with them nor did we share the same standards, morals and values.

I entered a relationship that I thought was everything I wanted in the beginning but here I am now, a survivor of domestic violence. DV victim, survivor or whatever technical term people like to use, I NEVER thought that would be me. Statistics show that victims of domestic violence can be of any race, age, gender. They can also be from any economic status as well. Bottom line people don't choose to be victims. EVER! It just happens. It's hard for me to write this right now but I have to because there's someone else out there that needs my story, that needs to know they'll get past this, that they will heal and will be okay.

Imagine being love bombed for many months in the beginning of your relationship. I thought this was the person I loved, trusted and cared about. But because he was not happy with how things were going in his life he started to change his attitude towards me, exhibit very toxic behavior and wouldn't leave me alone. At the end of the relationship things got even worse. He would call me out my name, harass me, literally wouldn't leave me alone and refused to let me go. He refused to let me be free and just live my life. I was in an very emotional state at the time. I felt like I had no control. I was being manipulated, lied to and mistreated one day and "loved" the next. I wasn't educated on the signs of domestic violence and didn't realize what I was in at the time.

The last straw was when he assaulted me. He assaulted me after repeated NOs and after repeated moments of pulling away. Assaulted me. He tried to take away my dignity, power and self respect.

I didn't know what to do. I was so gone and torn mentally. Luckily I spoke to the right person who let me know what I didn't know at the time. I was in an emotionally and mentally abusive relationship. Emotional and mental abuse led to sexual assault and I'm sure if I would have stayed, it would have led to physical abuse as well. This person would not leave me alone. For some reason he felt that I belonged to him so he wanted to control me. There were patterns and cycles of love and then the abuse. I didn't know what I was in at the time. When people are in these situations sometimes they are not aware, they don't know what they're going through, and think these unhealthy relationships are love. It's not because love doesn't hurt. Unfortunately, I learned that the person just didn't know how to love. Luckily I spoke to the right person at the time who let me know I needed to get help. I needed to get this person away from me. After being assaulted, I reached out for help.I finally had gotten this person away from me, but after that came the fear and trauma. Let me be clear- no one makes these things up for the fun of it. NO ONE!

Trauma. What's trauma? Google became my best friend during this time. I was experiencing a lot of feelings and emotions but did not have the name for it. I wanted to see a therapist so badly because I needed someone to talk to. After finally getting a therapist whom I could trust, I was diagnosed with depression, anxiety and PTSD. A girl like me- Pretty, soaring in her professional life, and in all other areas of her life, depressed? Diagnosed with PTSD? I knew life would never be the same. To make light of this situation, did you know Gabrielle Union-Wade, my sister in my head, was also diagnosed with the same thing after she was assaulted in a shoe store after work. She is now an advocate for survivors of sexual assault. Somehow knowing that someone else went through the same thing let me know that I wasn't the only one. Thank God that today I am in a happier state and have overcome these things.

To the men reading this, please treat women with respect. we are precious and pure. If you don't know how to genuinely love and don't have good intentions just leave her alone. Please, on behalf of all the woman in the world, I ask this of you, please.

Luckily today, I've moved passed this. This experience taught me how to forgive, taught me to be even closer to God, taught me how to love myself. It taught me how to heal, and helped me to become a wiser, stronger and more mature woman today.

As women in today's society, we go through a constant cycle of dealing with men who are undeserving of us. Guys who don't bring half of what we bring to the table, who are emotionally incompetent and just plain ol' ain't worth it. Undeserving because maybe he didn't have a better job, did not have the same drive, was mad that you made more money or insecure because of your beauty, or just insecure in himself. I write this to tell my story. Time heals all wounds. Believe it or not, as women we go through some of the toughest situations. This was one of the worst situations that I have gone through in my life, but I have overcome it and I am able to talk about it today.

Sometimes we can feel like we're the only ones and suffer in silence, but unfortunately this is apart of the journey as a woman encountering many frogs as I like to call them. Don't feel like you're the only one or it's your fault. Many men are intimidated by strong, independent women because of their own insecurities, fears and lack of self-esteem.

As you heal through whatever you're going through, take time. I've watched some of the most powerful and successful women in my life go through different horror stories involving undeserving men who wouldn't give them the respect and love they deserved for reasons that have nothing to do with them.

As you heal, find the things that you love about yourself. Remember those things. Think positive thoughts. Know that life will move on. Know that this too shall pass. Know that you will be okay and no matter what you do, work on knowing your worth and owning every single quality that makes you who you are.

Whatever it is, move forward. At the end of the day you're all you have and that's what matters most. Enjoy the time alone. Heal relax, take time and know that this too shall pass. Practice self-care, take time to watch your favorite movie, cry if you need to, write it out, talk to family and friends.

Notice signs of abuse as well as the signs of a healthy relationship. Visit The National Domestic Violence Hotline for a 24/7 hotline and https://www.thehotline.org/is-this-abuse/abuse-defined/ to be aware of the signs.

Chapter 13.

❦

Honesty

Some people lie to themselves and to other people about who they are. This is not a good practice because they won't be happy if they don't know and own who they truly are. As a teacher, I have spoken to my students in the past a lot about honesty. Being honest can be difficult at times but a part of self-love is knowing who you are at the core and being honest with how you feel.

I find it easiest for me to be honest with myself when I'm alone and I get time to process my thoughts. I get to figure out how I actually feel about everything. Even if I don't share all of my feelings with others, and you probably shouldn't, I'm taking the opportunity to be honest with myself, learn about myself and validate my feelings.

Ways to practice self -love and healing through honesty include:

☐ Meditating silently

☐ Meditating while reading or listening to the Bible

☐ Making voice notes to get out your feelings

☐ Using a meditation app such as headspace or peace

☐ Journaling

☐ Breathing exercises in peace

Being honest is a good practice and will help you to find peace and achieve self-love, healing and happiness. Find time to meditate and find time to decompress. Relax and get your mind right.

Also practice honesty with people. You can be honest with people about who you are and how you feel about certain interactions. You can be honest about what you like and don't like. Always walk in truth no matter what. Even if you don't feel comfortable sharing things with other people, make sure you feel comfortable sharing these things with yourself.

You can also talk to a therapist whom you can trust and get out all your feelings and emotions without guarding anything, without lying, and without having too much pride to say how you feel. Find someone you can be honest with about your feelings and emotions. If not, just talk to God, or talk to yourself. Get it out, write it in your journal. Practice being honest.

Chapter 14.

 ∾

Do Things You Enjoy

Take time to do things that you enjoy. Do things that are positive. What are somethings that you like to do? I love to go out with friends, dance, spend time with family at least once a week and I also love listening to music. I also love physical activities such as playing basketball, volleyball or even soccer. There are many things that I enjoy, sometimes I forget to tap into them and just enjoy life because I'm always focused on the next move or the next thing that has to be done.

Create a balance in your life. If you work five days a week, at least take the other two days to do things that you enjoy. It is also okay to do things alone. Some examples of things that you can do for fun are:

- ☐ Going to the movies
- ☐ Walking in the park
- ☐ Walking through a mall
- ☐ Playing a sport
- ☐ Dancing

☐ Partying

☐ Joining a book club

☐ Yoga

☐ Relaxing at home

Try to balance working, relaxing and socializing. Make time to go out even if it's taking yourself out on dates and make time to spend with friends and family. Cherish the time you have with yourself and do things that you love.

Enjoy things that are also healthy habits, such as going to the gym, reading, or meditating. Try making an effort to become more social and actually put doing things you enjoy on your to do list. A part of self-love and happiness is taking care of yourself physically and having a happy mental state. Put the phone down, enjoy the outdoors, enjoy the weather, enjoy people, do things that you enjoy.

. . .Work Hard, Play Harder. . .

Chapter 15.

❧

Stay Consistent & Make Sacrifices

I've learned in order to be successful, you need to be at peace with yourself. You don't want to have any bad energy. You want to always make sure you're real. Find peace within yourself. Know that this takes time. In order to be successful you need to also know that consistency is key. Consistency, hard work and discipline are what separate those who make it from those who don't.

It is said that it takes 21 days to build a habit. If you work towards what you want, you will see results. I want you to make a to do list, a list of things that need to be done today, tomorrow, later and someday. Practice organizing yourself and build consistency. Take at least three actionable steps per week for your goals. You'll notice you will begin to see results. You also need to learn how to make sacrifices. Even for me, being able to write this book took consistency and sacrifice. I had to take many weekends to apply myself and actually do the work because I knew that I had a goal and task that had to be done. Discipline is also important, self discipline makes the difference.

We are all now adults, will be transitioning into adulthood or even may be young adults. We need to own our responsibilities and get things done. We need to get in the mindset of being disciplined and making sacrifices; making sacrifices and doing things that are productive and that are helping us grow. If you have a goal, get it done. Stop entertaining things and people that are no longer serving you. Keep your focus and be a go getter. Be someone who does what they need to by any means necessary. If you need to take momentary breaks for a few days because life does happen, do that and get back up. Continue to make the sacrifices you need to make in order for you to be consistent and do what you have to do by any means necessary.

. . .Without struggle there is no progress. . .

Chapter 16.

~

Gratitude

So you've reached your happy place! What now? What's next? These are often the questions I ask myself instead of just learning how to be content. Often times, not being happy with the now and still wanting more, can lead us to a path of unhappiness. Use all that God has provided for you. Continue to create new visions, keep going and embrace all that you have achieved and be your best self.

Gratitude needs to be your attitude in order to appreciate and recognize all that you do have now. Be grateful for the little things. I remember days when I didn't have enough money to eat or just didn't have enough to do the bare minimum for myself. If you've ever had those days, appreciate the days when you do have enough. Focus on the things you have now instead of focusing on the things you don't have. This will help you to create a positive mindset and will help you to be happier.

Show more appreciation and live a positive life. You will be happy. Be thankful for the little things, thankful for a place to rest your head, thankful for a place and for food and clothing. Be thankful for the people in your life, for the ability to pay your bills and just for a new day and life. Even if you're not exactly where you want to be, know that this too shall pass and gratitude needs to be something that you practice in order for you to get more out of life.

. . .Count your blessing, in order to achieve more and be at peace and see what you have gratitude has to be the attitude. . .

Chapter 17.

⁓

Stay in Your Magic

There was a time in my life when I struggled with having self confidence. I use to be so worried about pleasing people and about what people thought about me instead of worrying and thinking about what I thought about myself. After doing a lot of inner work and soul searching, I'm fortunate to be grounded and I can confidently say I know who am I today. I'm confident in myself as a person, everything that I have accomplished and my attributes and abilities.

I believe that I have a soul and an ego. I believe your soul is who you are internally with no pride and your authentic self in spirit. I believe that our ego is who we are on the outside, who we present ourselves to be in front of others. Even though some people would speak against a person being egotistical, as women we have our ego for a reason. When you're around people, in social circles, in public or just outside, this is when it is necessary and okay for you to operate off of your ego. Always have a sense of humility but your ego is your sense of self esteem and self worth. It is okay to have pride, it is okay to have a strong sense of self worth, and absolutely necessary for you to stay in your magic. Being completely honest, when you're in certain spaces, not everyone is going to like you. You need to walk in a room and not wonder if people like you, but instead decide if you like the people in the room. Always wear your invisible crown, walk with pride, and keep your head high. Sometimes people will misinterpret your confidence for being cocky, but you need to love yourself, you need to walk with confidence because if you don't believe in yourself, stay in your magic and remain confident who else will? Believing in yourself also gives you power, it gives you power against those who may not take heed to you for whatever reason. Stay in your magic and be confident no matter what.

When you're on top, when you're in your prime, you will be tried and tested. But, if your confident, know your value and your worth, that invisible crown will not fall off. I was once at an event where we talked about the importance of networking and how it can be very intimidating sometimes even being in a room or in a space where there are other people who are just as strong and powerful as you. In these situations, you always want to be confident. Think about the qualities about you that make you shine. Think about what's special about you whether it is the way that you interact with people, the way that you're able to build relationships, or your authenticity. Maybe it's just your life experiences and the ability that you have to share your story. Make people aware of you, your qualities, your skills and experiences.

. . Be confident, own your talents & stay in your magic. It's a must. .

Chapter 18.

~

Your Circle Matters

Getting around the right people is the biggest success hack in the world. Never underestimate the importance of professional and personal relationships. You're not meant to do things alone. You should have a network and a circle of people that you can depend on both professionally and personally. If it wasn't for my circle, I wouldn't be the person I am today.

I think about my childhood friends, family, co-workers, college friends, acquaintances, mentors and coaches. All these people are the ones who help to uplift me and keep me going. It's very important to build relationships. It's not what you know at times but who you know. Your ability to be successful will be dependent on your work ethic and also your network.

On a personal level, it's important to build relationships and maintain relationships as well. I have to remind myself of this so often because I enjoy being alone, but we are social creatures. Maintaining a social life will help you to feel happy, loved and supported. My circle consists of family and friends from elementary and high school, friends that I hang out with socially. Also, friends that I've built a rapport with on a professional level and mentors and coaches. I also have friends that I have met through social organizations and I am blessed to have them all.

I would not have been the person that I am today without the relationships I've built and the people that I have in my life. Oftentimes we hear people say you are who you surround yourself with. At an earlier age I learned the importance of mentorship. I learned that a support system and a circle consists of everyone that you surround yourself with whether that is family, friends, co-workers, professional network, and also your mental and physical health care network such as a therapist and doctors. It's important to have a network of people that will support you. Your circle matters.

It is important that you surround yourself with people who are going to elevate you, uplift you and add value to your life. Surround yourself with people who are worthy of being in your presence and have the same values as you, that are like minded and that can make you a better person.

Don't be afraid to eliminate people out of your circle. Know that you will outgrow people and that is okay. You want to also surround yourself with people who are doing more than you, so they can push you to get to the level where they are. I know at times it can be intimidating, especially when we are inspired by or look up to a particular individual.

Since I was younger, I wasn't always the biggest people person. I was actually and still am very introverted. As I got older, I had to push myself to be around other like-minded women because I didn't want to do things alone. I wanted support and to have a sense of sisterhood in my life. I've continued to meet amazing women and people in general by joining different organizations on my college campus.

I joined professional organizations that were aligned with my mission of empowering and supporting women. I've recently joined Women by Choice and Pearls of Power and I'm looking forward to continue joining organizations even as I grow older. Sometimes as professionals, it can be hard to find people who are like-minded, so seek support from organizations, find mentors, coaches and sponsors. Go to events and network. Push yourself , your circle matters.

. . .It's not what you know, but you who know. . .

Chapter 19.

~

Keep Going & Reflect Often

Dream until your dream comes true. You need to know that everything you want can be manifested. Set a vision for the things you want in life and then work towards seeing them manifested. Take actionable steps and make sacrifices. Reflect on what you want or what is no longer serving you. Visualize where you want to see you self and work towards these goals. In 2018 I made a vision board for the first time. I put all of the things that I wanted to accomplish by the end of 2018. At the end of the year I accomplished all of those things and more.

In order to be a successful woman you need to be reflective. Have a vision for yourself and the things that you want out of life so you can work towards them. Take time to write down things that need to get done. Organize yourself my creating daily, weekly and monthly to do lists. Push yourself to get things done quarterly and keep yourself organized and motivated.

Reflect, keep going and reflect often. Sometimes we may be grappling in our spirit and not feel at ease because we're surrounded by situations and people that are no longer serving us. Sometimes we outgrow situations and people and we need to take time to mediate and cleanse our spirit to get a gauge of where you are physically, mentally, spiritually and emotionally in order to keep yourself happy. Know what things you need to get rid of in your life and what things you need to give your energy to. Keep going and reflect often.

. . .Reflection is one of the most underused, yet powerful tools for success. . .

Chapter 20.

⁓

Live Your Best Life

Combining all the principles you have learned such as being happy, being grateful for everything you have and have accomplished and learning to be at peace will help you to achieve the ability to live a happy life. You've learned all the strategies to keep you grounded, you know what it means to love yourself, you know how important it is to be at peace. Reward yourself and now go out and live your best life! You've worked hard, know that it's okay to play hard too. Be a social butterfly, have fun with your friends and build a social life.

Take time to do things that you enjoy. Have all of your friends come over or just simply enjoy the weather or watch a movie. We are all social creatures so it's important to have a social life. Isolating yourself can become lonely, so push yourself and get out there!

Life is short, make efforts to live more and worry less. Also take pride in yourself in order to live at your best. It is said that "Beauty awakens the soul to act". When you look good, you feel good. Take pride in your physical appearance. Take time to do those small self-care activities such as, getting your hair and nails done, shopping or taking time to sort out your favorite outfits. Your physical appearance matters. Take pride in it.

Once you're fully comfortable with yourself, you'll be comfortable around others. Think about the circle of friends that you have and make cherishable moments with them. Create and make memories, make an effort to make time for those who love you. As millennials you need to know you are in your prime. Now is the moment when you need to live your best life! Live more and worry less, know that God is in control of your life and sometimes we need to just simply have fun enjoy and live.

There are many things you can do for fun such as going to brunches, dance classes, exercising, partying, talking on the phone and enjoying your social media. Also spending time to shop and to take care of yourself in different ways and making sure to start booked and busy!

What are some things that you enjoy doing? What are some things that are on your list of things to do? Now that you've overcome all your trials, now that you've done the work, you've learned how to love yourself.

. . .Let go, forgive, relax and live your best life. . .

Book Synopsis

I like to think of myself as a two-sided masterpiece, from the outside looking in I look like I have it all together, but I have faced many obstacles in life.

No one posts their failures, how to overcome your failures and be a successful woman. In this book I share my story and how you too can overcome your trials and tribulations and turn them into triumphs.

Embrace Your Journey. Love Womanhood.

In A Journey into Womanhood, you will learn key principles that will help you to acquire success, happiness and self-love as you transition into womanhood. As I transitioned into womanhood, I learned key lessons that helped me to become the woman that I am today. As women we can look like we have it all together but, in all actuality many of us are women facing different battles and issues such as making poor decisions, having a lack of self-confidence, and not being satisfied with where we are personally and professionally.

In a Journey into Womanhood, you will learn how combat these issues, transform your life, and live a meaningful, happy and purpose filled life.

This book will teach you how:

·   To learn and know who you are and how to stay grounded.

·   To embrace your journey and transition into womanhood successfully.

·   To turn failures into opportunities and become a boss.

·   To overcome low self-esteem, lack of self-respect and truly love yourself.

·   To enjoy your adulthood, build relationships and live your best life.

In this book you will find:

Your key guide and principles as a young millennial to achieve success, happiness and self-love.

Embrace Your Journey. Love Womanhood.

--

Krystal Davy is currently an educator, author and speaker. She is also a thoughtful leader for today's millennial woman. She lives in New York City and is well known for her drive, purpose and transparency. She is the founder of Being A Phenomenal Woman, working to help young women live happy and healthy lives. To learn more about products and services visit www.krystaldavy. com

Facebook: Krystal Davy

Instagram : @KrystalDavy

Twitter:@KrystalDavy

www.ingramcontent.com/pod-product-compliance
Lightning Source LLC
Chambersburg PA
CBHW021204090426
42740CB00008B/1219